The Leader In The 2014 Mirror

By

Michael Camp

ISBN 978-0-557-52039-8

CONTENTS

"Focus on the things you do want to occur, not those things you do not want to occur."

TONY DUNGY

When I began my management career nearly twelve years ago, there was very little focus on self-development outside of trial and error. I never spent much time reading leadership books or became involved in mentor relationships to help me with my shortcomings. A few years ago, I read a leadership book called "Quiet Strength" by Tony Dungy which made an immediate impact on me. This book was one of the most interesting books I ever read and it motivated me to want to do more for my team.

In my first managerial position, I was responsible for one person and a small loss prevention program for a major retailer. Being new to the leadership role, I obviously struggled with how to properly lead instead of manage. As I worked through the next few years I began to develop a skill set which allowed me to better communicate with my team. The next management position I held was an Assistant Manager with a major retailer working outside of loss prevention and was responsible for more than one-hundred people.

This was definitely a new role that required me to learn a new set of skills. Even in this position where I directly influenced hundreds of people every week, I still had not developed the necessary skill set of changing from a manager to a leader.

One of the key learning lessons for someone new to a supervisory role is the importance of knowing these positions have a great deal of responsibility that comes with them. Each of us is blessed with the opportunity to influence others and help develop them into the leaders of tomorrow. One of the challenges for people in positions of responsibility is to fully understand there is a difference between being a leader and a manager. It is one thing to manage an area and deal with the day-to-day operations, however, it is a totally different responsibility to influence and develop those around you as a leader.

I have always enjoyed taking on new challenges and stretching my comfort zones, so I began writing leadership moments for my team members. These lessons were a simple one page story about some type of leadership skill I felt was appropriate for their development process.

Through the process of writing these lessons, I received positive feedback from those who read them and decided to continue this process. I truly believed if at least one person received something from these lessons, then they were worth my time writing them. Taking the time to develop those around me helped me gain an additional piece to the leadership puzzle I was facing. As a leader it is critical to continuously develop those around you today in an effort to build stronger leaders tomorrow.

Along with writing leadership lessons, I worked with each of my team members to create an Individual Development Plan (IDP) to address their strengths and weaknesses. The IDP process quickly identifies a person's strengths and weaknesses, while requiring an action plan to address them appropriately. One of the major focus areas for me over the past few years has been in developing those around me to ensure they are prepared for future growth.

When you are fortunate enough to be in a position to lead people, you must recognize the responsibility you have in developing those future leaders around you.

Leaders are not only expected to train and develop their successors, but should also share leadership lessons learned over the years. I hope you enjoy this book and can take some of the teachings with you in your day-to-day responsibility of leading those around. In the words of Albert Einstein, "A life lived for others, is a life worthwhile".

DEDICATION

To my wife Karren,

I wouldn't be the man I am today without your love and support.

To my children Madelyn and Benjamin,

Thank you for showing me how awesome it is to be a dad!

To my father Charles,

Thank you for being a great dad and for all of your support.

PART ONE

THE LEADER IN THE

MIRROR

"The quality of a person's life is in direct proportion to their commitment to excellence regardless of their chosen endeavor".

VINCE LOMBARDI

CHAPTER ONE

LIVING WITH INTEGRITY

"Integrity is that internal compass and rudder that directs you to where you know you should go when everything around you is pulling you in a different direction".

TONY DUNGY

When I think about the characteristics of a leader, the first one I think of is integrity. Having the responsibility for a group of people is difficult enough without having trust issues. The people around you have to know when you say something, you mean it. There is nothing worse than listening to someone speaking about something but knowing the odds of this being true are minimal at best. When you're trying to get the people on your team engaged and supporting the vision, it is critical to have a level of trust between each of you. When I think about the managers I worked for over the years, very few of these managers were actually leaders. Some of the reason why they wouldn't be considered leaders was due to the lack of trust they built with those working for them.

Without trust and integrity, a person is most likely going to struggle when it comes to getting those around them engaged in the program. A leader can build trust with those around them by living a life where honesty and integrity are paramount in their daily lives.

Whether you are dishonest concerning a small issue is no different than if you are dishonest when dealing with a large issue. I have always considered my integrity to be like an eggshell. An eggshell is delicate at times and should be handled with care. With each act of dishonesty, a small crack pierces the eggshell. Just like an eggshell, your integrity has a thin layer of protection before it is completely destroyed. Your integrity should be handled with extreme care, even on the small issues. Remember, once you get a crack in your eggshell, it is impossible to repair it. Some people believe that as long as they handle the big issues right, they can fudge on some of the small issues. This type of thinking couldn't be further from the truth.

I once read a quote which sums up the value of integrity and how important it is to possess this as a leader today. John Maxwell stated,

"Anytime you break a moral principle, you create a small crack in the foundation of your integrity". As a leader, each opportunity where you fail to maintain your integrity will be a moment never forgotten by those around you. I can remember the times when I knew my bosses weren't being honest with me and how these acts made me question their integrity. One way a leader can be viewed as not being honest is when they act one way towards some people, then act completely different around others. Regardless of whether an issue is minor or major, treat them all with the respect required and never let your integrity be questioned.

CHAPTER TWO

COURAGEOUS LEADERSHIP

"Difficulties mastered are opportunities won".

WINSTON CHURCHILL

Leading courageously to me, means someone who demonstrates courage both physically and morally, someone who takes responsibility for their actions and someone who shows a willingness to take risks. When you think of someone leading courageously, is there someone who comes into your mind quickly? When I think of someone who demonstrated courageous leadership, I quickly reflect on my father. My father was only seventeen years old when he enlisted for the United States Air Force in 1958. At the time of his entry in to the military, he was a just boy from a small town in Mississippi with only a high school education and a desire to defend his country. Within a few years of enlisting, he was sent overseas to support the Vietnam War. I can only imagine the fear, uncertainty and emotional stress he must have faced when he boarded that plane.

My father spent the next few years in Vietnam fighting for his country before returning home. He stayed in the military until his retirement in 1986 and proudly served his country for twenty-eight years.

We have all experienced situations of uncertainty where our emotions took over and we felt emotions like fear, anxiousness and sadness. However, when I think of courageous leadership, there truly is no other definition than that of a soldier who leaves their country to fight for our freedoms in an unknown land.

When you demonstrate courageous leadership to people around you, a level of trust begins to develop. If you take a moment to think about the best boss you've had the pleasure to work for, I am sure you have witnessed them demonstrating courageous leadership at some point. A leader, who has the integrity and courage to do what's right each and every time, will win over the support of their people. Courageous leadership comes from deep inside you and is not a learned skill. By showing courage when leading others, you will inspire those around you to perform at higher levels. As stated earlier, leading courageously is not something we can teach people. It is something deep inside each of us and we make the choice whether to exercise this asset or not.

14

The choice is yours, so when you get the opportunity to lead with courage, will you?

"A man's courage can sustain his broken body, but when courage dies, what hope is left?" Proverbs 18:14. You don't have to be the greatest leader in the world to be courageous; you just need to have the desire to be the best you can be.

CHAPTER THREE

DEFINING YOUR ATTITUDE

"Nothing can stop the man with the right mental attitude from achieving his goal; nothing on earth can help the man with the wrong mental attitude".

THOMAS JEFFERSON

Most people define attitude as the feelings they have inside that are displayed in their behavior outside. The attitude you display to others will impact every aspect of your life. When you have a positive attitude, you will project openness to those around you and people will want to follow you. On the other hand, when your attitude is negative, you project a closed image and most people won't follow you. Your attitude impacts everyone around you and plays such a large part in how people perceive you. So why wouldn't you want to be perceived in a positive light?

As leaders, we are responsible for developing the future leaders of our company. These people will mold their leadership style from behaviors and attitudes they witness from their previous leaders. We owe it to our Associates to show them what a true servant leader looks and acts like each and every day.

Your attitude can either draw people to you, or repel them against you. Have you ever met those people who always have an excuse when something doesn't work out the way they expected it to? Maybe they came to work grumpy and they blame it on the fact they woke up on the wrong side of the bed.

When they fail at things in life, they quickly say it's because of someone else, never them. The thing most of these people fail to remember is that we are responsible for our attitudes and we choose to be "grumpy" or "angry" when things don't go right for us.

When I hear the word *attitude*, here is what I think a leader should display:

A – Appreciation for their team

T - Treat people fairly

T - Think about others first

I - Invest in the future of their team

T -Teamwork always

U -Understand the needs of others

D -Develop trust with their team

E -Empower their team

Your future and the futures of those in your circle of influence will be impacted by the attitude you display. You owe it to yourself and those around you to display the most positive attitude you can. There is nothing worse than to work for someone who displays a negative attitude and doesn't inspire you to do anything above the norm. On the other hand, how awesome is it when you work for a leader who truly inspires you and make you want to be more than you are, simply by how they treat you.

CHAPTER FOUR

INFLUENCING OTHERS

"Whatever words we utter should be chosen with care for people will hear them and be influenced by them for good or ill."
BUDDHA

It is an outstanding opportunity for us to be fortunate enough to make an impact on the lives of so many people in our roles as leaders. Some leaders don't truly realize the number of people they influence, either negatively or positively, each day. The least outgoing person in a leadership role will still influence thousands of people in their lifetimes. Imagine the number of people you can influence if you were outgoing and really took influencing others seriously. I can think of only a couple of leaders in my career who have made a positive influence for me, while the list for negative influences is quite extensive.

When I think about the leaders who have made a positive impact with me, the characteristics of these leaders were very similar. Each of these people had a skill which allowed them to communicate easily with others and all were genuinely good listeners. They also possessed the skills of being a compassionate person who took the time to care for others while accomplishing the mission at hand.

We've all experienced the boss who would only give you half of their attention while doing something else. The impact made on someone when they are not taken seriously or feel like they are not important, is definitely a negative influence. Negativity breeds negativity, so it becomes even more important to influence people in a positive manner to keep your staff fully engaged and inspired.

A story which truly exemplifies how leaders can positively influence others is the story of Tony Dungy, former head coach of the Indianapolis Colts. In Tony Dungy's book "Quiet Strength", the future Hall of Fame coach describes how he continuously rose to the top after each failure. After completing four years at the University of Minnesota as a Big Ten quarterback, Tony knew his chances of becoming an NFL quarterback were pretty good. Over those four years, Tony won multiple awards and his performance was outstanding. With all of these accomplishments in college, a total shocker came when Tony never received a phone call on draft day. It was rumored the reason he was never drafted to play quarterback was due to the color of his skin.

This was obviously a blow to Tony's confidence, but he didn't let it deter him from his goal of playing football in the NFL.

Tony finally signed with the Pittsburgh Steelers and played for Coach Chuck Noll. Tony's determination to never give up, regardless of the obstacles he faced and his tenacity to always do the right thing truly made an impact on me. Throughout Coach Dungy's career as a player and coach, he has faced obstacle after obstacle with the style and character of a true leader. Coach Dungy has a unique ability to teach and mentor at the same time, while engaging his players to do the uncommon.

Coach Dungy distributed a handout to his players in an attempt to encourage and teach, and here is what it said.

"The first step toward creating an improved future is developing the ability to envision it. VISION will ignite the fire of passion that fuels our commitment to do WHATEVER IT TAKES to achieve excellence. Only VISION allows us to transform dreams of greatness into the reality of achievement through human action. VISION has no boundaries and knows no limits. Our VISION is what we become in life". (Taken from "Quiet Strength", by Tony Dungy)

What an inspiring message for those players to receive, to see how their vision had to become a team vision and how they all must commit to ensure excellence. As a leader, you have a unique ability to influence those around you in so many ways. If you choose to be a leader who motivates and inspires others, you will most likely leave a lasting positive influence on people. On the other hand, if you choose to be a leader who barks out orders and fails to appreciate those around you, the influence you leave will most likely be a negative one. My challenge to you is why would you want to leave a legacy of negativity when you're gone?

CHAPTER FIVE

BUILDING TRUST

"Few things help an individual more than to place responsibility upon him, and to let him know you trust him."

BOOKER T. WASHINGTON

Whenever I think about relationships I have been blessed to have throughout my life, one common bond is always there. Trust is the foundation of any relationship and when trust is broken, it is like having a house sitting on bad foundation, which is never a good thing. As we build relationships with people in our lives, each of us begin to trust those people to a certain degree and become accustomed to what we believe these people stand for. When one of these people acts outside of the "perceived" image we have of them, the level of trust is impacted. If the act committed is a serious lapse in judgment, the crack in the foundation of trust will be permanently altered. I am sure you can think back through your career and quickly identify when someone you respected did something which impacted the level of trust between you.

Unfortunately, for the person who broke the trust, these memories never go away.

Former U.S. Representative, J.C. Watts defined integrity and character in a pretty clear manner, "Character is doing the right thing when nobody's looking. There are too many people who think that the only thing that's right is to get by, and the only thing that's wrong is to get caught". When it comes to building trust with others, this process takes time and cannot be built overnight.

Building trust takes time and must be done with a patient hand to ensure the end result has a strong foundation. For me, the words integrity and trust go hand in hand. You cannot have trust with people if they don't feel like you demonstrate integrity or don't display your true character. It is extremely important to gain the trust and respect from those around you in order to be successful. Failure to gain the trust in these relationships will prove to be a key factor in whether or not you succeed with your goals.

Most people would rather work a job they don't like than work for a leader they can't trust.

Trust has been proven over time to be a key skill necessary for leaders to take their teams through challenging times and be successful. When I think about the word trust, I visualize the following foundation being built one brick at a time:

Brick 1: **T** – Think of the needs of others before your own.

Brick 2: **R** – Relationships must be genuine.

Brick 3: **U** – Unconditional respect for everyone, everyday!

Brick 4: **S** – Stand strong in the face of adversity.

Brick 5: **T** – Take responsibility for your actions.

By delivering on your promises and by standing strong in the face of adversity, you will start to build the level of trust necessary for a leader to be successful. Take time today to think about those relationships in your life and start building a solid foundation of trust.

METHODS TO DEFINE THE LEADER IN THE MIRROR

1. Leaders must maintain their integrity at the highest levels.

2. Don't make excuses for your behavior.

3. Adversity is tough, stay strong, and your true character will prevail.

4. How you get there is just as important as getting there.

5. Responsibility is tough. Your courage is critical to success.

6. How you influence others is extremely important. Be a good role model.

7. Be true to yourself. Don't be a "yes" person.

8. Be responsible for your actions. Have courage to stand up when you should.

9. Your attitude impacts others. Be a positive impact!

10. Respect people for what they do, not for what they are.

11. People may not listen to everything you say, but they will see everything you do.

12. If you don't like the leadership image in the mirror, change it!

PART TWO

BREAKING FREE FROM

YOUR COMFORT ZONE

"We shall have no better conditions in the future if we are satisfied with all those which we have at present."

THOMAS EDISON

CHAPTER SIX

TAKE ON NEW CHALLENGES

"It is time for us to stand and cheer for the doer, the achiever—the one who recognizes the challenges and does something about it".

VINCE LOMBARDI

Most of us prefer to keep a schedule, a certain flow to their day, and a career path which makes us feel the most comfortable. No matter how old you are, everybody gets nervous to some extent when it comes to making changes which take them out of their comfort zone. When we talk about breaking out of your comfort zone, what does that even mean? Well, for most of us, it simply means taking on challenges where your abilities will be stretched and you test your skills in a new arena. Facing these challenges is scary and leaves most people with a sense of uncertainty with anxiety.

The majority of people in this world feel comfortable when things are familiar within the following groups: family, geographic location and daily activities. When there is no familiarity within these groups, we began to feel nervous about the situations surrounding us.

With this nervousness, there is uncertainty of whether or not we wish to continue in this environment. During these turbulent times is when a true leader pushes forward and faces the challenges of potential failure due to uncertain conditions.

As a brand new military recruit, I can recall the uncertainty I felt when my bus arrived at Lackland Air Force Base in April of 1991. Not knowing for sure what I was about to embark on, the emotions of uncertainty and possible failure entered my mind. While facing these challenges, there were most certainly moments of stress and nervousness, but I pushed forward in an effort to stretch my comfort zone. I remember a phone call with my father on day three discussing the stress and uneasy feelings I experienced. He told me to stay focused and to observe things around me so I could get a better understanding of my environment. He said there may be stresses related to facing new challenges but the rewards for facing these challenges outweighed the stress. I took his advice and faced my fears, and within no time, I felt more comfortable in my new environment.

As you go into the future, career development will be one of the most critical weapons you can possess in your arsenal.

Not taking chances or testing your skills will most certainly leave you in a field with little to no advancement possibilities. A few ways to break out of your comfort zone can be as simple as taking on "tasks" your boss typically completes, or asking for projects you know nothing about. Whether you seek advancement in your career, or just want to achieve a personal goal, the critical point will be whether or not you face the challenge of stretching your comfort zone. Will you make the right choice and stretch your comfort zones? Or will you be left in the past clinging to the comfortable situations surrounding you? The choice is yours.

CHAPTER SEVEN

SET ASIDE YOUR FEARS OF FAILURE

"I know fear is an obstacle for some people, but it is an illusion for me…failure always made me try harder next time".

MICHAEL JORDAN

Almost certainly, a variety of great tasks await you in the future. Facing these challenges, we have the possibility of being afraid to tackle them. Some of the reasons we are fearful of approaching these challenges are due to the fear of not being able to recover if the attempt is a failure. Making mistakes is a part of life where if we choose to learn from them, we are more likely to be successful in the future. When you make a mistake, the important thing to remember is to learn from it and get back to business. If you sit around thinking about the mistakes made and how bad they were, you will build up a level of fear which may paralyze you from moving forward.

If you want to achieve these challenges, you must plan for the success. If you simply dive into the challenge without proper planning, it will most likely not achieve the results you had in mind.

We have all tried and failed at least once in our lives, so making mistakes shouldn't be the end of the world. However, proper planning should be a simple decision for you, especially if you've acted abruptly in the past with poor results.

When you make mistakes, it is critical to get back up on your feet and think about this strategy to move forward with your challenges:

M –Manage your emotions.

O –Observe the mistake to identify any lessons learned.

V –Visualize what you want to achieve.

E –Erase the mistake from your memory, but remember the lessons learned.

F –Formulate your goal with a detailed plan to ensure success.

O –Obtain the necessary tools for the completion of this challenge.

R –Recruit others to assist with the challenge.

W –Welcome mistakes and the experiences they provide.

A –Acknowledge the need to make changes to your original plans.

R –Review your progress frequently and make necessary adjustments.

D –Determine a way to measure the success of the challenge.

If you stay engaged, stay on the plan and continue to get back up when you get knocked down, you will achieve any challenge you take on! Making mistakes is just a part of life and we all make them. There is no reason to get so bogged down with every mistake made, just learn from them and prepare better next time. Thomas Edison failed over 1,000 times before inventing the light bulb and was fired from two jobs for being unproductive. He made mistakes but never gave up hope or his passion for success.

METHODS TO BREAK FREE FROM YOUR COMFORT ZONE

1. Don't be afraid to learn something new.

2. Challenge yourself to face your fears.

3. Make a mistake. Learn from it. Forget about it.

4. Plan for what you want to happen.

5. Know that you're going to fall short sometimes. Keep the faith.

6. Be positive in your attitude, it impacts others too.

7. We all fail. The key is how we handle failure and respond to adversity.

8. There is nothing wrong with getting knocked down; it's the getting back up part which counts.

PART THREE

SERVING OTHERS FIRST

"The measure of a leader is not the number of people who serve the leader, but the number of people served by the leader."

JOHN C. MAXWELL

CHAPTER EIGHT

A LIFE LIVED FOR OTHERS

"Everybody can be great, because anybody can serve. You don't have to have a college degree to serve. You don't have to make your subject and verb agree to serve. You only need a heart full of grace, a soul generated by love.

MARTIN LUTHER KING JR.

As leaders, we are fortunate to have the opportunity to serve the needs of others above our own. For some, the opportunity to serve unselfishly comes easy, while it is a struggle for others. I believe we all possess the desire to serve others; it becomes a matter of whether or not we choose or find the time to do it. When a leader chooses to put the needs of others first, they show a commitment to the development of those around them. The servant leader is truly rewarded when those they serve reach their full potential, begin to perform at their best and start to serve others as well.

It's easy to say how important servant leadership is, but without a full understanding of what it looks like, a leader could struggle. A servant leader will possess characteristics which will clearly show their commitment to the growth of others.

When I look back over my career, there are some obvious leaders who demonstrated a clear message of servant leadership. As I reflect on the actions of the leaders in my past, a few characteristics come to mind.

S – Shows empathy by learning the needs of others to better understand how to lead them.

E – Empowers their Associates.

R – Respects those around them, always!

V – Visualizes beyond the day-to-day concerns and looks at the big picture.

A – Actively listens to the concerns and needs of others.

N – Nurtures the spirit of those around him or her. Always tries to help others develop.

T – Team player attitude; always willing to pitch in when needed.

I keep a quote from Albert Einstein taped to a shelf at my desk, it says, "Only a life lived for others, is a life worthwhile." When you read those words, it becomes clear to see what it takes for us to truly call ourselves Servant Leaders. When those people around you think of your leadership style, would they call you a servant leader?

What do you think they would say about you? If you haven't demonstrated servant leader qualities to those around you on a consistent basis, then you probably wouldn't like their answers.

To truly serve others and put their needs above your own, here are some of the things you should be doing.

- o Truly support the development and growth of those around you.
- o Share responsibility for failure but also give credit for successes.
- o Take a genuine interest in the lives of those around you.
- o Listen to their needs and assist whenever possible.
- o Build genuine relationships with coworkers, customers, and friends

When given the opportunity to serve others, will you show the strength to steer away from self-serving leadership and demonstrate the respect and motivation for serving others? As leaders we are only as valuable as the people around us, and we are responsible to take care of these people as well. Putting others first will always add value to your leadership legacy and will add value to those you serve as well.

CHAPTER NINE

ARE YOU A TURTLE HELPER?

"The many of us who attain what we may and forget those who **help** us along the line we've got to remember that there are so many **others** to pull along the way. The farther they go, the further we all go."

JACKIE ROBINSON

When I think about being a leader, another important aspect is the development of others. As leaders grow, so must those around them if they wish to remain successful. A leader cannot afford to focus solely on their own development while neglecting those who may be needed in the future. Some leaders are fearful of teaching too much to those around them for fear of creating more competition. This approach is absolutely the wrong choice and failing to develop those around you is only a recipe for failure.

In a book titled "The Maxwell Daily Reader", John Maxwell shared the story of Alex Haley, the author of "Roots", who kept a picture in his office of a turtle sitting atop a fence post. Mr. Haley kept it there to remind him of a lesson he had learned years before:

"If you see a turtle on a fence post, you know he had some help." Haley remarked, "Anytime I start thinking, 'Wow, isn't this marvelous what I've done!' I look at that picture and remember how this turtle (me) got up on that post."

Developed leaders and those who developed them are very similar to the turtle. The unique view from the fence post is made possible by others assisting us. When I think about the story of the turtle and how it made it to the top of the fence post, I can't help but be reminded of the times I was able to see that view with the help of others.

As a new manager with very little experience leading people, I struggled at times with the process. I was fortunate to have leaders in my path who were "turtle helpers" and were willing to spend time to help develop me as a leader. One leader comes to mind right off the bat, his name is Jim Farinelli. Jim had a unique ability to communicate to his staff in a way which was non-threatening and was able to get results with this approach. In a world where some leaders get results with negative actions, Jim was a maverick and chose to go the other way.

When I first arrived at the office, I struggled with the dynamics of corporate America. Jim took the time to develop me instead of reprimanding me. Had he chosen the other route, it could have led me down the wrong road. The leadership lessons I learned while working for Jim have continued to assist me in my role today. I am certain I would not have enjoyed the view from the fence post had it not been for Jim's ability to see my struggles and know how to handle them. He always took the time to visit with me and provide guidance rather than barking out orders or reprimands. His leadership over the years has been invaluable to my growth and I am certain his "serve others first" mentality has helped me become a better servant leader today.

Take time to think of those "turtle helpers" you have experienced in your career and thank them for their assistance. Remember to develop those around you and enrich their lives so that one day you may be referred to as a "turtle helper".

METHODS FOR SERVING OTHERS FIRST

1. Always show a genuine concern for others and their development.

2. Put the needs of others ahead of your own.

3. Empower those around you to do more.

4. You have two ears and one mouth for a reason. Listen more than you speak.

5. Strive to make a difference in the lives of others every day.

6. Don't ask people to do something you wouldn't do.

7. Develop strong relationships built on trust and respect.

8. Show them how to serve and they will follow.

PART FOUR

EMPOWERING YOUR TEAM

TO DO MORE

"As we look ahead into the next century, leaders will be those who empower others".

BILL GATES

CHAPTER TEN

BUILD A DREAM TEAM AROUND YOU

"Surround yourself with the best people you can find, delegate authority, and don't interfere".

RONALD REAGAN

When you observe a successful person, it seems simple to think they made it to the top on their own. We all know when someone rises to the top; they inevitably had help from more than one other person (probably a turtle helper). A leader must assemble a team where each person possesses certain skills and strengths the leader does not possess. With each person on the team having their strengths, the entire team will be more successful and diverse. This in turn will elevate the leader of this team to more opportunities down the road, because as we all know, a leader is expected to get results.

Leaders are paid to deliver the numbers… no excuses and no exceptions. When a leader doesn't take the time to assemble a strong team around them, they won't have as many opportunities to perform at their highest level.

A leader's potential to perform is closely related to the strength of those surrounding them as a supporting cast. If a great coach has players who are not committed to the game plan, regardless of the coach's talent, the team will not be as successful as they should be. Building the supporting cast is critical to the success of the team. One mistake some leaders often make is surrounding themselves with people they like or people just like them. When building your dream team, put serious thought into what you really need, not what you really want.

So, have you assembled an all-star team around you? If not, what are you waiting for? In the words of Mother Teresa, "You can do what I cannot do. I can do what you cannot do. Together we can do great things". John Maxwell shared a poem by Ella Wheeler Wilcox in his book "The 21 Irrefutable Laws of Leadership" which sums up the importance of selecting specific people to be on your team.

> *There are two kinds of people on earth today,*
> *Just two kinds of people, no more, I say.*
> *Not the good and the bad, for 'tis well understood.*
> *That the good are half-bad and the bad are half-good.*

45

No! The two kinds of people on this earth I mean,

Are the people who lift and the people who lean.

There two kinds of people on earth today;

Just two kinds of people, no more, I say.

Not the sinner and saint, for its well understood.

The good are half-bad and the bad are half-good.

No; the two kinds of people on earth I mean,

Are the people who lift, and the people who lean.

Make certain to select the right people for your team and continue to develop them. It is critical for a leader to have a skilled team around them and to keep sharpening their skills in an effort to help them reach their full potential.

CHAPTER ELEVEN

CONTINUOUS DEVELOPMENT

"Even if you're on the right track, you will get run over if you just sit there".
WILL ROGERS

Throughout our life we have experienced cycles of learning which have prepared us for the events in the future. Some life lessons are critical to survival while others are simply experiences we wish to avoid in the future. When we experience these life lessons, we generally take something from this learning and add it to our life skill sets. The successful leader will take all of these lessons and develop their skill set to ensure future success. At the same time, a successful leader will teach these lessons to those around them as a development tool. Sharing experiences and knowledge to others is paramount to the growth and development of your team.

In my current role, I am fortunate to work for a leader who truly believes in making her team better by empowering them to do more and by focusing on the development of others. When I think about empowering others and the positive impact it places on people, I recall a personal experience I was placed in a few years ago.

47

My boss asked me to take on a very large project dealing with a subject I knew nothing about. This project was going to take me out of my comfort zone, but this leader had faith in my abilities and shared this confidence with me.

Simply knowing my leader had confidence in me and the fact she shared her influence, I was able to complete the project with great results. This experience taught me the importance of believing in your people and how critical it is to share your influence with them. Having faith in others and inspiring them to take on more challenges will make those around you better than ever.

When you empower others, you change their lives and both of you will experience a positive impact on your personal and professional growth. Some leaders don't like the idea of giving away their authority because they think it takes something away. In fact, by giving away your authority to others, you increase the ability of others without decreasing yourself. This is truly a WIN-WIN situation that will make you a better leader!

As important as it is to develop others, you must remember to develop yourself as well.

We all know what happens to things that just sit there and don't progress. If you fail to update your skills or fail to challenge yourself to learn something new, you too will become outdated. One important part of self development is the use of an Individual Development Plan (IDP) to identify strengths and weaknesses of your current leadership style. An IDP is a process of asking those around you to identify your top three strengths and the top 3 weaknesses you may have as a leader. The best feedback will come if the people feel like you are serious about their comments and are willing to make necessary changes based on their feedback.

By taking a serious look at the way you lead, you will identify shortcomings and highlight the things you do well also. Continuous development is like planting vegetables in the garden. Once planted, these vegetables need continuous watering and care if you want them to develop into the end result. A leader needs this continuous watering as well, in the form of development. A plant that stops getting water will stop growing. A leader who stops learning will stop growing as well.

Some people are not comfortable asking others for feedback on their leadership skills and the feedback may be difficult to hear at times as well.

However, the honest feedback gained from your peers, those who report directly to you and your immediate supervisor will prove beneficial in your progression as a leader. So if you truly are passionate about making the "leader in the mirror" an image to be proud of, you will need to place a strong emphasis on your development. Without seeking the input from those around you, it is almost impossible to know exactly where your weaknesses truly lie.

So when you are developing your leadership skills the focus should not to outbid someone else, it should be for the betterment of you. William Faulkner says it best when it comes to your development, "Don't bother to just be better than your contemporaries or predecessors. Try to be better than yourself."

CHAPTER TWELVE

MOTIVATING THOSE AROUND YOU

"It's not the will to win, but the will to prepare to win that makes the difference".

PAUL "BEAR" BRYANT

As leaders, there are times we need to motivate our Associates and other times when we need to ensure we avoid things which de-motivate them. So many times we worry about the right way to motivate our Associates, but fail to remember the importance of common mistakes which could do more to damage Associate motivation than we think.

I am sure each of us has experienced those people in our lives who were great motivators and had the ability to get people to do extraordinary things. A true sign of a strong leader is someone who can get the "troops" engaged with the plan and motivate them to accomplish the unexpected. There have been many famous leaders who have possessed this unique ability to motivate others. When I look back over my career there was one leader who possessed these skills more than any other. Her name is Debbie Hodges. She possesses strong communication skills and has the ability to keep people engaged in the plans.

Debbie was able to challenge me to take on more than I thought I could handle and above all, she is an honest leader. With these skills, she was able to take a group of leaders and challenge us to dream higher than we had before and to accomplish things we never thought were possible. By accomplishing extraordinary things, my confidence level grew which also made me a better leader.

So many times we worry about the right way to motivate our Associates but fail to remember the importance of common mistakes which could do more to damage Associate motivation than we think. Here are a few mistakes to avoid when trying to motivate others:

1) Providing inconsistent leadership to those around you

Changing workplace rules too frequently or failing to communicate these changes to the team, or by breaking promises to those around you. Most people aren't willing to put forth the extra effort if they can't depend on their leader's words to be truthful. As leaders, it is invaluable to have our actions display what our words are saying; this helps to maintain a strong trust with the team. Inconsistent leadership only confuses those around you by not letting them feel comfortable with what kind of leader they have.

2) Offering vague praise to those around you

It always feels good when your boss says "Good Job", but it doesn't necessarily tell people what they did specifically that was viewed as good. If a leader gives this type of vague praise to everyone, then the "go-to" people might not feel the need to work any harder than anyone else. Leaders are trusted by those around them, so the words coming out of their mouths will be evaluated and vagueness will come across as insincere.

When offering praise to those around you, remember the three B's, 1) be specific, 2) be sincere, and 3) be consistent. Insincere gestures only lead to questions about the integrity of the leader, which ultimately leads to trust issues with the team.

3) Failing to appreciate the work of those around you

It's easy to get lost in the cracks of a large company and to feel like your role is not important at times. People are less likely to work hard when they don't have a sense of encouragement and importance from their leader. When people don't feel important, they tend not to associate value with doing a good job. Showing those around you how important they truly are will help keep them fully engaged and it will also show them how much you care about them as well.

I read a quote by former Pittsburgh Steelers head coach Chuck Noll about the power of motivating those around you which truly defines the importance of positive motivation. Coach Noll says "The mercenaries will always beat the draftees, but the volunteers will crush them both". After reading this quote I began to think about what this means in the corporate world. Mercenaries are paid for their services and rarely will they develop emotional bonds between themselves and the job at hand. Mercenaries (or people who are paid) can be effective due to the money motivation, but this effectiveness will be short lived. Draftees tend to enter into these situations with an attitude which reflects a lack of commitment, because let's be honest, they probably don't want to be there to begin with. Draftees (or people who are forced to do something) are usually not very effective. On the other hand, a volunteer generally doesn't care about the money and they almost always develop an emotional bond with the job because their hearts are engaged. So when it comes to those around you, are they mercenaries, draftees, or volunteers?

METHODS FOR EMPOWERING YOUR TEAM TO DO MORE

1. Be sincere and provide honest feedback.

2. Motivate your team to do the unexpected.

3. Provide continuous development opportunities to stretch their skill sets.

4. Set an example and inspire others with your actions.

5. Live your life with honesty and integrity always.

6. Make those around you think they're better than they are.

7. Recruit volunteers! They really want to be there.

8. If you have mercenaries on your team, find a way to change their motivation or let them go.

9. Lead in a way that inspires people. Avoid leadership traits which net you a team filled with draftees.

PART FIVE

RECOGNIZING OTHERS

"People often say that motivation doesn't last. Well, neither does bathing, that's why we recommend it daily".

ZIG ZIGLAR

CHAPTER THIRTEEN

SINCERE APPRECIATION FOR OTHERS

"Appreciate everything your associates do for the business. Nothing else can quite substitute for a few well-chosen, well-timed, sincere words of praise. They're absolutely free and worth a fortune".

SAM WALTON

One of the basics to winning the support of those around you is to appreciate them for their efforts. Everybody likes to receive positive feedback from their boss about their work performance and some even like it to be done in front of their peers. When people are appreciated, they immediately feel valued. When you appreciate people in front of others the gesture increases in value with peer recognition. People also need to be given the credit when they perform well on a project, keeping mind that public recognition is even better. My current boss assigned me to work on a large project which would impact a wide range of stakeholders. At the conclusion of this project, she took the time to appreciate me in front of a group and I can tell you it meant the world to me.

Sam Walton, former CEO of Wal-Mart Stores, Inc. had a unique ability to motivate his Associates. One way was by appreciating them for their efforts. When Mr. Sam walked into a store, he would call the Associates to a section of the store and visit with them. During these conversations he would always show his appreciation for their hard work and dedication to the company. When Associates received this public appreciation they would be re-energized and worked even harder the next time. When a leader takes time out of their schedule to show sincere appreciation for the efforts of those around them, everybody wins. Whether you give out certificates of appreciation, trophies for performance, or just a (hand written) thank you note, those around you will feel valued and respected for their contributions to the team.

Most people find it difficult to work for a boss who doesn't appreciate the person or their performance. When a leader fails to make the people around them a priority or fails to provide the appropriate recognition for hard work, the effect will be detrimental to the success of the group. People love to be appreciated and recognized for their contributions. We all like to know when we have done a good job.

The most common mistake for new leaders is a failure to recognize the efforts of those around them.

Leaders who fail to show this appreciation could cause their people to feel undervalued and disgruntled. We can all think of times in our careers where we experienced a boss who failed to show appreciation or recognition. When you reflect on these experiences, I am sure the overall feeling in your mind is negative. You probably ended up leaving those jobs as well. I've heard the comment, "people don't leave jobs they leave people"! Leaders must have the ability to know when and how to provide appreciation and recognition to those around them if they want to be successful.

How long has it been since you took time to provide sincere appreciation for those people on your team? What are you waiting for?

CHAPTER FOURTEEN

MAKE OTHERS FEEL IMPORTANT

"People will forget what you said; people will forget what you did. But people will never forget how you made them feel".

JOHN MAXWELL

One of the most important things I do to appreciate those around me, is to make people feel important. Making others feel important is critically important to maintaining a high level of engagement with your team, and it also keeps motivation levels high. How you make others feel important is as different for each person as the people are themselves. What I mean by this is the process of how you make them feel important can vary depending on the personality you're dealing with. For some people, when you give a simple "thank you" with no public accolades, it works for them. For others, remembering important events or people in their lives means the world to them. In my daily practice I try to find someone around me and appreciate them for their work and try to make them feel special. If you look, it's much easier than you think.

In my current role, I supervise approximately 190 people and interact with hundreds more every day.

During these interactions I learn things about each person and what things they like to do in their spare time. I also mark their birthday on my calendar and try to send them a birthday greeting (usually in the form of a Power Point presentation) on their special day. I pay attention to the moods of those around me and when I notice someone may not be feeling well, I send them a message to brighten their day. Remembering important life events or the fact their child plays a specific sport, can lead to conversations about their personal life, which also helps build the trust between a leader and those around them.

When a leader takes time to learn about the person and shows an interest in them, the bond between boss and employee grows. When those around you feel like you care about them, they are more than willing to work their best and achieve more. The quote from John Maxwell says it all, "People do not care how much you know, until they know how much you care".

I experienced the value of making others feel important first when I was shopping with my family.

My new Vice-President, Debbie Hodges had only been in our department for a few weeks and we had only spoken a few times prior to meeting her in the store. Debbie immediately came up to my family and began having a friendly conversation. My little girl was six months old at the time and Debbie asked if she could hold her. Debbie immediately began making the baby faces and speaking in baby talk to amuse my daughter. At the same time directly behind Debbie was her new boss. We made eye contact and I said hello to him.

With this being said, I am sure Debbie heard who I was talking to but she didn't budge. Most people new in their position would have easily forgotten about me and my family to engage in a conversation with their new boss. Debbie never lost contact with my daughter and the conversation never swayed during those brief moments when I said hello to her boss. At this point, Debbie was showing me how my important family was to her at that moment.

METHODS TO RECOGNIZING OTHERS

1. Give credit to others when achievements are met.

2. Appreciate those around you in public forums.

3. Make sure the appreciation is genuine and deserved.

4. There is nothing worse than giving generic recognition.

5. Spend time to learn about people and get to know them.

6. Reward excellence and celebrate together.

7. Acknowledge the potential of others.

8. Share successes with those around you.

9. Make those around you feel valuable.

10.Put the needs of others above your own.

11.Don't just say how important people are, show them!

PART SIX

NAVIGATING THE RIGHT COURSE

"On the road of life, a good leader always has a road map".
MICHAEL CAMP

CHAPTER FIFTEEN

UTILIZING YOUR G.P.S.

"A leader knows when to drive and when to let others take the wheel".

MICHAEL CAMP

Many of us are given assignments and we typically go into these with a strong intention of completing it. Sometimes, we may not be able to execute the assignment due to some type of roadblock or distraction. These roadblocks can be of the physical or mental form which can keep you from achieving your goals by distracting you from the plan. As a leader, you must be able to appropriately address roadblocks you face and have alternate routes mapped out.

Anytime I have planned a vacation, which required many hours behind the wheel of a car, I would plan out the trip to the finest detail. I would ensure I knew the exact roadway to take, how long it should take to get there, that I had all of the supplies necessary for the trip and obviously, I would ensure the vehicle was prepared for this long journey. It seems funny to put so much effort in planning a week long vacation on the road.

65

However, so many people don't think a life long journey as a leader needs a detailed plan. Unfortunately for me, only after making some mistakes did I realize how important the road map for my leadership success truly was. After facing this realization, I sat down and plotted out my road map and developed my G.P.S.

For me, the term G.P.S. has two definitions in my life. The first one is an electronic device in my vehicle which provides clear directions for me so I won't get lost. The second is a detailed approach to my career which, if used properly, will also provide clear direction and keep me from getting lost. The second G.P.S. stands for Goals / Plans / Strategies. If you take the time to visualize where it is you want to go, simply input the data into your G.P.S, sit back and enjoy the ride.

Some leaders may not feel the importance of a detailed road map and like to fly by the seat of their pants. Failure to properly plan for the future can lead you to take multiple wrong roads in your journey causing you to face road blocks and ultimately delay your arrival.

If you want to visualize what causes you to detour from your objectives, you must identify what potential "road blocks" look like. Here is a brief breakdown of things to do to keep personal roadblocks from making you take a detour from the planned route.

- o **Keep your eyes on the road; not on the billboards.** Make sure to keep your mind clear of mental distractions in order to keep your field of vision on the road. If your eyes are constantly looking side-to-side, how can you see what's coming up ahead?

- o **Your map may not be clearly defined, so use your G.P.S.** (Goals. Plans. Strategies). Some leaders fail to plan properly with a detailed outline of what it will take to execute the assignment. Failure to utilize your G.P.S. appropriately will certainly lead you down the wrong road and will make your trip more difficult. Former NFL coach Herm Edwards once said "A goal without a detailed plan is nothing more than a dream"!

- Make sure to focus on the basics, such as "check the oil".
  All assignments have boring pieces which sometimes don't receive the attention necessary to ensure proper execution. As with checking the oil in your vehicle, checking the fine details (the basics) of the assignment will ensure you get where you're going successfully.

- Know when to be the driver and when to be the passenger.
  A good leader will know when to take on the assignment and when they need to properly delegate. It is critical for each of us to know when our plates are too full to adequately execute an assignment and when to bring in other drivers. Plan your time and delegate properly to ensure your plates aren't full, thereby causing a roadblock.

When it comes to planning the long journey of your leadership career, make sure to take time and visualize what roads you want to take. Starting down the road without a detailed map will most often lead the driver into unfamiliar territory and cause delays.

CHAPTER SIXTEEN

SETTING REALISTIC GOALS

"Setting a goal is not the main thing. It is deciding how you will go about achieving it and staying with the plan".

TOM LANDRY

In business today, it is essential to have a strong vision for the future and a detailed set of goals to ensure success. If you think about the times in your life where you wanted to achieve something important, you most likely spent time preparing to ensure success. Having a dream and aspiring to attain this dream is not enough to ensure you get there. It is mission critical to have a detailed plan with S.M.A.R.T goals if you wish to achieve your plans.

In order to put together your goals, using the S.M.A.R.T. system will benefit not only you but those around you as well. Goals should be Specific, Measureable, Attainable, Realistic, and Timely. When you think about a goal being specific, it should clearly state what you are ultimately trying to achieve. Simply saying I want to achieve is not enough. When we say the goals should be measureable, we mean there should be a way to measure your success on whether you achieved the goal or not.

69

Goals should be attainable, not some pie in the sky goal which is utterly unachievable. Realistic goals are simply that. These goals should be viewed as real, not something where achievement is unlikely. Last but not least, a goal should be timely. You will need to put a timeline on the accomplishment of the goal. A goal without a deadline will be harder to achieve.

Another part to having realistic goals is to ensure they are easily understood by those people tasked with helping you achieve them. When you have a clear vision and detailed, thoughtful goals, you will ensure the "buy-in" from those around you. When you gain the support of your team, goal completion is much more likely to occur.

People want to follow strong leaders who have a clear vision of what they want to accomplish together. The people around you want to know they are all working as one team on one agenda, together. When a leader is able to gain the support of those around them, anything is possible. We can always achieve more when we act and think together because it allows a diverse thought process which is always a good thing.

I can remember my first management position where I was in charge of a small group of people and was not very good at goal setting. In the beginning I struggled to accomplish all of the tasks in a timely manner and when I began accomplishing these things, it was simply a checklist without a vision. I am sure those people around me viewed these tasks simply as that, with no real vision, which must have been frustrating for them. In a few months I was able to sit down with my manager and discuss these frustrations and she helped me understand the importance of setting a clear vision and formulating my goals. It was difficult at first to determine what my true goals were and with her assistance and a lot of scratch paper, I was able to write down the top three goals I wanted my team to achieve for the year. When I shared my vision and goals with my team, I couldn't believe their response. Each member of the team seemed to have a little more bounce to their step, their productivity increased and morale improved.

At the end of the year, my team was able to achieve all three goals set in the beginning of the year and we celebrated the team's success. The next year, I communicated with my team and we set the top three goals and I gained the "buy-in" from everyone because they viewed it as a team process.

71

Along with setting clear goals with those around you, it is critical to share your vision as well. As we manage people every day, it is easy to get caught up and forget to lead with a vision instead of simply managing people. There is an absolute difference between a manager and a leader, and it begins with having a clear vision. Taking the time to think about what your vision should be is not a process which occurs overnight. If a vision is put together too quickly, it can unravel and cause those around you to lose their trust in your leadership. When developing your vision, it is helpful to talk with mentors and leaders you respect to get their concepts on what a vision should be. After you gather information from others and develop your vision, the next step is communicating this vision clearly to those around you.

Communicating your vision is almost as important as creating the vision itself. Having a great vision but failing to communicate it properly, can lead to some people choosing not to follow you. Successful communication of your vision occurs when all members of the team clearly understand their role, their responsibilities, and their accountability for failing to meet the goals and timelines.

The players need to understand why you think the way you do, the reasons you have determined the goals and expectations and most importantly, they need to know they can trust you. When leaders communicate effectively with those around them they are viewed as trustworthy.

When leaders withhold certain information, it can have a negative effect on the team when it comes out. A leader won't earn praise for attempting something and failing, and is judged by the success they bring to their group. John Maxwell says, "Your success is measured by your ability to actually take people where they need to go".

When I think about a leader who had the ability to clearly communicate their vision to a large group of people, the name Sam Walton comes to mind. Mr. Sam had a unique skill where he could clearly communicate his thoughts about the company to anyone he visited with. His vision clearly stated he wanted to provide a quality product to people at a discounted rate so they could live a better life. When Mr. Sam discussed these thoughts with his Associates, he was able to gain their trust and ultimately their "buy-in". With his vision clearly communicated to those around him, Mr. Sam became one of the most successful CEOs in the history of the world. **73**

The people around him knew what he expected from them and together they accomplished what no other company had done before. This vision is still alive and well within Wal-Mart and the company continues to achieve goals that seemed unachievable at times.

In the words of James Lane Allen, a nineteenth century American Novelist, "Dream lofty dreams, and as you dream, so shall you become. Your vision is the promise of what you shall one day be; your ideal is the prophecy of what you shall at last unveil".

CHAPTER SEVENTEEN

NAVIGATING THROUGH ROUGH WATERS

"Anyone can steer the ship, but it takes a leader to chart a course".

JOHN MAXWELL

A previous boss once told me, "It's easy to lead people when times are good, but it takes a strong leader to do it when times are bad". This statement has come to ring true even more over the past few years as we have all dealt with the economic issues facing our country. A strong leader doesn't allow the elements around them to change the way they think, act or respond to issues. When those around the leader see them responding during critical times, it is very important for them to see a composed leader they can trust. We have all experienced stressful situations where we probably didn't respond in the correct manner and hopefully, we learned something from these situations. The problem is when those around you see you struggle repeatedly during stressful times; they will have a tendency to lose faith in your ability to lead. The best leaders are able to motivate their teams to do the unexpected and accomplish things even though they may face fears during the adversity.

Leaders continually develop as they go through adversity and depending on how they handle the crisis will determine whether they develop up or down. When you think about those defining moments in your career, how did you handle the crisis? Would the leader in the mirror be proud? If not, hopefully you realized the leadership lesson in the moment and took time to think of a better response to the situation for future reference

When you think about how you respond to critical moments, does a feeling of easiness come to mind? Do you thrive and perform better during difficult times? If you don't, then here are some things you can do to help become a navigator in your business:

N –Never make decisions when you're frustrated.

A –Always demonstrate a calm demeanor to those around you.

V –Visualize what outcomes could be possible.

 I – Include others in the decision making process whenever possible.

G – Gather all of the facts first.

A – Analyze the data and take time to think it through.

T – Take action.

O – Outcome should be communicated to those impacted.

R – Remember that your actions are being watched by those around you.

When you take the necessary time to think through critical issues, you will demonstrate the leadership skills required to effectively lead others. We have all worked for those people who jump too fast when making decisions and usually they end up backing up and attempting it again. When this occurs, the faith and trust between the leader and the followers will suffer. As leaders, we must have the forethought to diligently review all of the information and make thoughtful decisions which impact others. Failure to properly execute during stressful times will undoubtedly lead to a panic situation where most leaders will not perform at their best.

We all want to follow a leader who possesses the strength and courage which inspires us to do more and without these traits, a leader will surely struggle. The former head coach of the Pittsburgh Steelers, Chuck Noll, once stated, "Leaving the game plan is a sign of panic, and panic is not in our game plan".

The challenge for a leader is to ensure they respond appropriately during critical times and when they don't respond correctly, apologize for the error and move on. There is nothing worse than a leader who makes bad decisions and never admits when they are wrong or make mistakes. We have all seen how people react when the "spotlight" is on them; usually the results are not favorable. If you are a leader who doesn't make good decisions during those rough waters, the image in the mirror most likely isn't one you are proud of. Make the efforts today and become a better navigator for those around you as well as for yourself.

METHODS TO NAVIGATING THE RIGHT COURSE

1. Stay calm and think problems through.

2. Always present a positive attitude even during crisis situations.

3. Don't go at it alone. Utilize your resources when making decisions.

4. Include your team when plotting the course.

5. Build strong relationships with those around you.

6. Take time to properly plan for the road ahead.

7. If you're not an explorer, take your GPS.

8. Remember that the decisions you make today could define your legacy tomorrow.

PART SEVEN

LEAVING A LEGACY

"A life isn't significant except for its impact on other lives".

JACKIE ROBINSON

CHAPTER EIGHTEEN

ADDING VALUE TO OTHERS

"The bottom line in leadership isn't how far we advance ourselves but how far we advance others".

JOHN MAXWELL

When I think about the role of a leader today and whether or not they are successful, it comes down to a few priorities. A successful leader will be someone who can inspire those around them to get things done, be a person of influence who has the ability to build strong relationships, and lastly, possess the ability to take others with them to the top. It's not impossible for a leader to make it to the top and fail to bring others with them, but what a lonely accomplishment that would be. A true servant leader will not only get to the top, but they will have the courage to support those around them so when they arrive, they won't be alone. Which type of leader are you?

As I thought about this chapter, an overwhelming feeling came to me about how fortunate I have been to work with leaders who added value to others. When I say you should "add value to others", I simply mean you should make those around you feel valued. A leader can add value to others by being a good listener and sharing information with those around them.

81

Another way to add value is to harness the potential of those around you in order for them to perform above expectations. Value everything about the people around you and take a genuine concern in their personal lives, as well as their professional careers. When you have conversations with people, do you always talk about yourself?

A leader with charisma will always listen to others first before talking about their personal issues. Would you be considered a charismatic leader? If not, take a look at how you communicate to others during conversations. If the conversation tends to focus on you and your interests, try listening a little more and speaking a little less.

In my career, I have been blessed to experience some outstanding people who have taken a personal dedication to my development. One person who stands out among the others is my father, Charles Camp. My father always took interest in my activities and was supportive, no matter what the endeavor. When I was a young boy, my parents divorced and I lived with my father and sister. While working in the United States Air Force, my father also held side jobs to ensure my sister and I had the things we needed.

The work ethic I learned from my father was quickly put into action when I began working in my teens. Regardless of the adversity facing my father, he always made me feel valued and took the time to teach me to become a better person.

I can recall visiting with my father when I was promoted to my first position in management and was asking for his advice. One of the things he told me has stuck with me and I still use his wisdom today. He told me a leader is responsible for those around them not just to ensure the job gets done, but to develop these people to do even more. I didn't really understand what he meant at first, but over the years we had additional conversations about how a leader should treat people and how a leader is blessed to be able to influence so many people. My dad took the time to add value to my life and to teach me the things which I truly believe have made me who I am today.

I can only hope the people who I influence every day will have a similar story about my leadership style. The leader who adds value to others will know they are successful when the people they influence start adding values to others lives as well.

A strong leader has the confidence to assist others without the fear of being outshined. I have worked for people who wouldn't help you because they feared you would take their job. This style of leadership not only hurts those around the leader, but it hurts the leader as well. A good leader will always stay close to their people and will remain connected to them regardless of position or title. Some leaders think because they hold a "higher" position, they are better than those not in these positions. This kind of leader couldn't be more wrong.

I recently viewed an email written by a leader which was addressed to the people reporting to him. The original email asked for volunteers during a specific time period to help with a community involvement activity. The leader wrote the second email because some of these people failed to respond to his request for help. The second email went a little something like this:

If you are receiving this email it is because you <u>failed</u> to respond to my earlier email.

I have two questions for you, 1) have you ever told someone to do something and they didn't do it? And 2) what accountability did you give that person? Then the email went on about failing to respond to these requests could be detrimental to their career and how their peers would view them differently. He also said "since you are only hourly employees, I cannot force you to volunteer. At the end of the email he goes into a barrage of negative toned comments about their lack of leadership maturity, etc.

I could not believe what I was reading. The fact a leader would ever communicate this way to the people around them made me disgusted. After reading this, I immediately contacted this leader to discuss his email. During our conversation, I discussed the role of a leader and how everything we do influences those around us. I told him I understood he was frustrated with their failure to respond to his first email, but there was another way to handle this. I continued to have a learning lesson with this leader and tried to express how this simple email could tarnish a reputation which took years to build.

As leaders, we must be cognizant of how we communicate and how the data is received by those around us. Everyone is entitled to be frustrated and make mistakes, but a strong leader will always stop to think about their words before losing their temper.

At the conclusion of the conversation, he apologized for losing his temper and for sending such a hurtful email. I told him he shouldn't apologize to me, however, there was a group of people he needed to apologize to and try to regain their trust. I can only hope he took to heart the conversation we had. I hope he can learn from this mistake and truly value those around him in the future. Because as leaders, we should feel blessed to have the opportunity to influence so many people and along the way, if we do it right, they will influence others too.

CHAPTER NINETEEN

SIGNIFICANT VERSUS SUCCESSFUL

"Do all the good you can, by all the means you can, in all the ways you can, to all the people you can, for as long as you can".

JOHN WESLEY

Many leaders today spend so much of their time trying to be successful and they forget how important it is to be significant too. It doesn't take much to be considered a successful person in today's terms. You can be defined as successful for simply obtaining a position which pays well and has good benefits. When you think about the word successful, what does it mean to you? In the world today, it seems like the word successful is thrown around a little too frequently that it has lost its value. On the other hand, the term significant hasn't been used as much as it should be.

When you treat people correctly, the impact you make on their lives should be eternal. The person who is able to get tasks accomplished while serving those around them will always be viewed as significant versus just successful. The question you have to ask yourself is will I be remembered as successful or significant by my family, friends, and co-workers?

I can tell you the most important thing for me, is to be remembered as a significant husband by my wife and a significant father by my children. What's important to you?

I was in a meeting once and a senior leader discussed how pleased he was with the performance of his team getting involved with the community. He said we all have a lot of work to do, but he was so blessed to work with "significant" people. He went on to discuss the importance of living a significant life versus living a successful one. This leader also went on to discuss how everyone in the room would be considered successful in most people's eyes, but there were some leaders in the room whom he viewed as significant leaders.

What a message this was coming from someone in his position and I can tell you, the people in the room got the message. A learning lesson I took away from this meeting was how important it was to stay focused on living a significant life and try to impact as many people as possible.

As a dedicated person wanting to do the best I can for my organization, at times I put my work as priority number one. After a few years, I finally realized by putting work first, I was putting my family second. **88**

In those first few years, I was promoted a couple of times and received many awards for my performance. While being considered successful in my early career, I wasn't being a significant husband. The importance of a work / life balance is absolutely critical to your personal development. A leader who fails to place things in the right priority will face the consequences in the end. I can remember my father getting on to me for working too much and he said, "Who would you rather have at your funeral, your co-workers or your family"? This really hit me hard and from that moment on, I made a change to live a significant life, rather than a successful one.

A leader needs to understand the importance of the work / life balance and know when the pendulum should swing to the other side and when it should stay in the middle. You won't always be able to attend the ballgames or dance recitals, but it shouldn't be that you never make them either. This balance was hard to figure out when I first was promoted and to be honest, it is still hard to decipher at times as well. Knowing when to trust the message coming from your heart is a defining moment in the life of a leader. When you get that moment, will you respond with significance?

Earlier we discussed if you make it to the top and you don't take others with you, then you did it wrong. The same message applies when it comes to influencing others around you. If you become a successful person but fail to be significant to others, you have missed the most important part of your journey. As leaders we have been blessed with the opportunity to build up others and influence people by the thousands. When in a position of leadership, why not take the challenge and influence as many people as possible in a positive manner. We can all look back on people in our lives to identify those who made such an impact and it actually changed how we behaved. When your career is over and the long work days are gone, will you leave a legacy to be proud of? Will those people you influenced practice the things you shared with them? There is more to life than working long days and making a lot of money, but at times it is difficult to see it.

Make sure to take time and appreciate those around you for their performance and take the time with your family to ensure the balance of work and life stays in line.

When you make it to the top, would the leader in the mirror be proud of

what actions took place to get you there? If the leader in the mirror is not

the leader you want to see, change that image now!

CHAPTER TWENTY

COMMUNICATION IS THE KEY

"The way we communicate with others and with ourselves ultimately determines the quality of our lives".

ANTHONY ROBBINS

How many times have you communicated something to a group of people thinking they would take it one way, and it ended up going the other way? So often in life we try to say what's on our mind and we end up communicating something else entirely. Even worse when you get the message out, it gets received differently by those around you. I once heard someone say, "Your output is someone else's input". This becomes pretty clear when you begin leading others. Failure to get your message across in a discernable manner will ultimately lead to confusion and possibly morale issues. As discussed earlier, leaders are judged by their words and their actions every day.

You can witness this type of leadership blunder any day on the local news coverage of politicians. I have viewed numerous times when a leader says something and the tone in which it was stated controlled the outcome of the news versus the content of the message.

How you say something means more than what you say most of the time. With this being said, the manner in which you speak to those around you will identify the kind of legacy you will leave. Have you stopped to listen at the words coming out of your mouth lately? If not, you should take some time and listen carefully to the words and tone you use when communicating to those around you.

When I think about communication blunders committed by leaders, the usual suspect is the tone used. Most people can take constructive criticism and guidance if it is delivered with the appropriate tone. A perfect example of tone causing more of a problem than the message is when a police officer stops you for speeding. I am sure we have all been stopped for speeding in our lives and for some of us, a little more frequently than others. Most of us were guilty of speeding when we were caught and are okay with getting the ticket, even if we didn't want to pay for it. What usually makes the ticket experience more personal than business, is when the officer has a bad tone or attitude.

When the police officer pulled you over to communicate the issue with you, how was their tone?

If the officer spoke down to you with rude tones, the experience most likely left you feeling more agitated with them versus getting the ticket. If the officer spoke to you with respectful calm tones, then the experience was better. The challenge is how do you speak to those around you when attempting to correct their behavior? Do you speak down to them like the officer in the first example? Did you speak with respectful tones and display a pleasant attitude?

The manner in which you communicate things and how you are perceived will ultimately determine whether or not your leadership style is viewed well by others. It seems simple enough to tell people how they should speak to others, but some leaders just don't get it. I use the old philosophy that you should speak to and treat people as if you had to spend the rest of your life with them in a very small room. It seems so simple to communicate to each other in a way which is comfortable for both parties, but so many times we choose the form which suits us best. When this occurs, the usual outcome is negative for the "listener" and tends to cause issues because of the tone or nature of the communication used.

When it comes to communicating effectively, I find this acronym illustrates the main points the best:

C- Clearly detailed messages will ensure affected people understand the message.

O- Open up the lines of two way communication with those around you.

M- Make certain the content of the message has the appropriate tone.

M- Manage your emotions, regardless of the message content.

U- Unintended body language can mislead people listening to the message.

N- Never make things personal, keep them professional.

I- Include the thoughts and views of others whenever possible.

C- Continue to listen more and speak less.

A- Attitude determines outcome!

T- Tones set the stage for how your message is perceived.

E- Everybody appreciates being spoken to with respect.

When you get the opportunity to speak with people around you, take the time to listen more than you speak and treat them the way you like to be treated.

These simple phrases seem easy to understand but unfortunately, they are the most commonly forgotten by leaders when communicating messages to those around them. When you have conversations or provide direction for others, would the leader in the mirror be proud of the words coming out of your mouth? If not, change your behaviors now.

METHODS TO LEAVING A LEGACY

1. Remember that the decisions you make today will define your legacy tomorrow.

2. Focus on identifying people who are capable of taking on more responsibility and give it to them.

3. Build strong relationships! At home and at work!

4. Look in the mirror and identify the leadership behaviors in the mirror you don't like. Then change them immediately.

5. Develop those around you to do more.

6. Remember the words you use today will define your legacy tomorrow.

7. Keep the communication clear and leave bad tones and attitudes at the door.

8. Identify and start developing your successor today!

9. Challenge yourself to live a life for others.

CONCLUSION:

IMPROVING THE LEADER IN THE MIRROR

We all start at different places within our leadership cycle so there is no cookie cutter approach to developing the "best leader". All you can really do is truthfully admit your shortcomings, focus on your strengths and work hard to develop the image you want the world to see. The challenges will continue to face you over the years and the secret to success is not always whether or not you handled each one properly. The secret to your success will lie on how you respond to failure and setbacks, and whether or not those around you feel like you are a leader they can trust. At the end of our careers we all strive to be remembered as a leader who did their job well and took care of those around them.

In part one; we discussed the importance of developing the leader in the mirror by focusing on the following areas: living with integrity, courageous leadership, defining your attitude, influencing others, and building trust. Each of these components is critical to master when in a position of leadership if the leader wants to be successful. If a leader fails to possess any skill mentioned above, there could be a recipe for disaster.

In part two; we discussed the importance of breaking free of your comfort zone and setting aside the natural fear of failure. A leader must possess the confidence necessary to make decisions with no fear of failure, knowing full well there is a chance to fail. The strength a leader summons during critical times and how they respond to mistakes made will ultimately define their leadership legacy.

In part three; the idea of putting others ahead of your self was discussed focusing on being a servant to others. I've heard it many times over the years the phrase "It's a dog eat dog world", well I disagree with this when it comes to leadership. The people working around you should know and feel comfortable with the fact they have a leader who puts their needs first. When people get this support, there is nothing they can't accomplish and the leader will ultimately accomplish more at the same time. Remember, you didn't get to where you are all by yourself, be a turtle helper.

In part four; the topic of empowering others to do more and building a strong team around you was discussed. We have all worked for the leaders who made us better by challenging us to do more without fear of failure.

The best coaches in any sport are always known as being great motivators and having a unique talent to get their stars to be even better than they already are. The leader inside you must have the ability to engage and inspire those around you to do more and to do it better than ever!

In part five; we discussed the need to recognize and appreciate those around you with sincerity. A leader who fails to appreciate the work of others will soon feel the effects of bad morale and poor productivity from the people around them. Make sure to visit with your team and build those relationships / partnerships which will get the members of the team feeling important again!

In part six; the discussion focused on navigating the right course as a leader and avoiding common pitfalls during the "rough waters" of leadership. We all have a built in G.P.S. which will guide us to the appropriate destinations, but we have to enter the data into it first. Setting realistic goals and developing a plan will aid in the input of this information so the team will arrive at the appropriate destination.

Finally in part seven; we discussed the importance of leaving a legacy where the leader could be proud.

Being called a leader is a privilege and therefore, it should be treated as such. When a leader adds value to others and understands the importance of proper communication between team members, a leader becoming significant is much easier to achieve. A leader can be successful, yet not be remembered as being a significant person by those around them. Getting things accomplished or achieving a certain goal is absolutely a good thing to strive for. However, when a leader truly understands their role, they will seek to become significant to those around them in exchange for only focusing on being successful.

With the tools you have in your leadership tool box, will you be able to build a leadership legacy worth remembering? Only you can determine the roads you will take and whether or not your G.P.S. can help you get there. Take time today and reflect on your leadership style, solicit feedback from those around you, and make a commitment today to change the leader in the mirror!

Made in the USA
San Bernardino, CA
16 January 2014